Fishing Bass-Ackwards

Coming Down the Pike with Off-the-Walleye Humor

Fishing Bass-Ackwards

Coming Down the Pike with Off-the-Walleye Humor

by JACK OHMAN

To my son, Eric,
who was given two fishing rods
even before he was born

ISBN 1-57223-030-4

Published by   WILLOW CREEK PRESS
                  P.O. Box 147
                  Minocqua, WI 54548

For information on other Willow Creek titles,
write or call 1-800-850-WILD

Printed in the U.S.A.

Contents

Acknowledgments

Is it possible to acknowledge every single person you've ever gone fishing with? Probably not, although my dad would undoubtedly figure in here somewhere. He thinks we never catch any fish together. He's still mad at me for the time I accidentally unhooked a large northern pike in 1972 with my brilliant net-handling prowess. For his birthday this year, I bought him a net the size of a handball court. My conscience is now clear.

My brother Jim has gone fishing with me when he's been forced into it at rodpoint. I am grateful to him for those times.

I'd have to throw my Uncle Hal in here, too. He had a little trailer on the Strawberry Reservoir in Utah up until not too long ago, and I spent many happy childhood days trolling for big trout, some of which I caught. I spent a lot of time fishing with Mark Strand, who is a real fishing writer and has actually caught huge fish, backed up by irrefutable photographic evidence. This book has stolen about 457 of Mark Strand's jokes. He can send Willow Creek Press a bill.

Dick Thomas and I have occasionally lifted them out of there, although not often enough. I fish — not enough — with Jim Ramsey, who fishes too much, in my estimation. I have fished with these people and many others, including Phil Cogswell, who likes to see his name in print. I will be eternally grateful to Bob Landauer for hiring me, and for encouraging me to fish when I begin to get inkblots on my corneas.

I gratefully acknowledge the editing skills of my wife Jan, who knows a lot about plural possessives. My agent, Jeanne Hanson, is accorded all due respect here.

JACK OHMAN
Portland, Oregon

Author's Note

I have deliberately excluded, mostly, any mention of trout, except when it was absolutely necessary to make a joke at, say, an entire state's expense. I included the steelhead, which is a trout, but is almost in a fishing category unto itself, because I'm from the Northwest. However, there are trout jokes and trout cartoons and trout references until the cows come home in *Fear of Fly Fishing*, my previous fishing book, which I recommend to the reader, for personal as well as financial reasons.

Also, I actually do enjoy fishing, although some whiny asides in this book may indicate otherwise. Just kidding, folks.

Introduction

Why do we fish? That's a question best not asked when you're sitting in a 12-foot aluminum boat that acts as a large convection oven in the 92-degree heat, and you suspect that the lake may be biologically dead. Still, the question remains.

Fun? Oh, right, fun. It's real fun to accidentally put a barbed hook in your cuticle and then pull it out with the precise surgical assistance of your drunken boatmate. It's loads of fun when you pick up your tackle box — you never listened to your dad, who always reminded you to keep the latch locked — and have its contents cascade onto the boat floor. It's buckets of fun to spend the next 30 minutes separating the Mister Twisters from the Lazy Ikes and the busted Zebco 202 you've been meaning to throw out but never do, not to mention the 17 nautical miles of Berkeley Trilene all wrapped around several thousand hooks, swivels, leaders, tweezers, De-Liars, and unidentified objets d'art. Lots of fun.

So why else do we fish? Relaxation? It's terribly relaxing out there on Lake Mille Lacs, bobbing up and down on six-foot swells like the Andrea Dorea, hoping that the boat doesn't just slip under the next trough, waiting for a walleye to latch onto your black leech and Lindy Rig. The rain is rapidly filling the boat, and you're making quick calculations about how long it's going to take — at the present rate of downpour per square foot per minute (three gallons, or so) — to sink you and the boat and your damned leeches, which you would swear are laughing at you. You're trying to decide whether to try to empty the cooler and hang on to it, or test out the kapok in your life jacket, which last felt water in the Swing Era. Real relaxing.

Maybe we fish because of the companionship of other fishermen. But let's be honest: would you invite over to your house the guy on the next boat cushion who smells of the following aromatic fragrances?

Aqua Velva, baloney, CheezWhiz, Cheetos, Uncle Josh's Bullhead Treets, three-day-old boxer shorts, Jack Daniels, a laundry hamper for the Green Bay Packers, Swisher Sweets, Old Spice, old dog hair, Old Milwaukee, carp gills, bass dorsal fins, a badly-tuned lawnmower engine, dead nightcrawlers, minnows that have been left in the sun all day, crappie lips, and leech entrails?

Of course not. You wouldn't want this man in the next state, let alone your happy home, where sanitary people live and eat. Not in a million years.

But we do all these things — willingly, enthusiastically — in the dogged pursuit of those slimy yet seductive creatures, compelled to spend thousands of dollars and devote hundreds of hours to their capture and even their release. Fishing — why do we do it?

This book will not answer that question.

But having told you about the positives of fishing, it is now time to move on to the soft white underbelly of fishing — the stories you never hear when vaguely malodorous people get together and lie about their catches.

So stand in the shoes of the fisherman.

But make sure he didn't accidentally leave the worms in them.

Fishing Bass-Ackwards

Know Your Enemy

The Sunfish

The sunfish is the entry-level prey for the neophyte angler. Sunfish congregate in schools of two to three million around docks or pilings, and can be caught by merely beckoning to them in a medium-high whiny voice: "Heeerrre fissshhheee fissshhheee fissshhheee" ... They rate below oak trees in relative intelligence, and swallow the hook down to their anal vent. They're kind of cute, for fish.

- NICKNAMES: Bream; Pest; Get Off My Hook You Little Dork.
- SIZE: From the size of a quarter to the size of a half dollar.
- COLOR: Greenish.
- EASE OF CAPTURE: A TV anchorperson could catch one just by thinking about it.
- LEVEL OF CHALLENGE: Fights like a pit bull for three quarters of a second, then it's like reeling in an Oreo cookie (no frosting).
- DESIRABILITY: Not as desirable as a crappie, but better than a bucket of uncleaned suckers.
- EDIBILITY: Tastes like whatever you put on it. You want chocolate sunnies, cinnamon sunnies? Go for it.

The Crappie

The crappie is what Good Ol' Boahs Down Sowf go fishin' for when they can't get the Largemouth Bass — in their parlance, Bucket mowfs — to hit. Crappies school in numbers that have not been replicated on our most sophisticated computers or even intoned by Carl Sagan. Crappies will hit jigs and live bait. Crappies have notoriously delicate mouths, so be careful: set the hook too hard and some poor crappie will swim liplessly for the rest of his life. You don't want that on your conscience.

- NICKNAMES: Speck; Papermouth; God, Not Another One.
- SIZE: Size of a shirt button to a deflated regulation pro football.
- COLOR: Phosphorescent off-green with black speckles.
- EASE OF CAPTURE: Have brains the size of a microchip. No problem. Use a cane pole for added rustic feel.
- LEVEL OF CHALLENGE: Like reeling in a sheet of notebook paper (lined, with holes).
- DESIRABILITY: More desirable than bullheads or radioactive carp.
- EDIBILITY: Tastes like the bottom of a lake with relaxed EPA standards.

The Bullhead

The bullhead is not really a fish. It's a kind of bottom-dwelling, trilobitish, tentacled ... object, I guess ... that takes bait as a real gamefish would, but is about as aesthetic as an effluent treatment facility. They're revolting. Bullheads and cockroaches will rule the world after nuclear war. Do not ever deliberately attempt to catch a bullhead as they have a rare and incurable curare poison in their slimy little whiskers. Who knows how much fishing carnage and unnecessary bait changes these little sacks of crud have caused? Try not to think about them.

- NICKNAMES: Bleecch; Yuck; Blauuuggghhh.
- SIZE: They're all the size of a Tootsie Roll.
- COLOR: The color of a Tootsie Roll.
- EASE OF CAPTURE: Easier to catch than rocks. Of all kinds.
- LEVEL OF CHALLENGE: Fight like Tootsie Rolls cut into thirds.
- DESIRABILITY: I wouldn't exchange needles with them.
- EDIBILITY: People have eaten bullheads thinking it was a way to commit suicide.

The Catfish

The catfish is a larger version of the bullhead. Why anyone would want to catch an incredibly large bullhead is beyond the realm of Western thought. It is not beyond Southern thought, however, because misguided people in our sub Mason-Dixon area of the United States avidly pursue these disgusting and frightening fish/feline monsters from Hell. Catfish are caught with blood-soaked rags and used tires covered with Dippity-Do. They are caught at night, which is probably just as well, because you would have to be treated for post-traumatic stress disorder after you looked at them in daylight.

- NICKNAMES: No known nicknames.
- SIZE: From about the size of your pinkie to the size of a Yankee Class Soviet sub.
- COLOR: Dark muck.
- EASE OF CAPTURE: Not too hard, considering they can kill you with their bullwhip-length tentacles.
- LEVEL OF CHALLENGE: Fight like caterpillar tractors in twelfth gear.
- DESIRABILITY: I wouldn't bring one to the prom.
- EDIBILITY: Spray paint them first to enhance eye appeal.

The Carp

The carp is not technically a fish. It's really a mammal — a cross between a pig and an otter — that happens to spend much of its time in the water. Carp don't really know how to swim; they kind of wallow like swine in soupy, wateresque venues like swamps and drainage ditches.

Carp are bottom feeders, like bullheads and members of Congress. They prefer junk food when they can get it. Frequently, carp can be observed with their exposed backs sticking out of the water, and appear to almost come up on land. In fact, carp have been known to survive for days in the woods, foraging for food and raiding campsites. In 1986, a 78-pound carp was shot and wounded in the South Bronx while on an extended foray above the surface of the East River; the carp evaded police SWAT snipers and stole several Sno-Balls and Ding-Dongs before returning to his natural habitat. Authorities are still looking for the carp.

- SIZE: From the size of a loaf of bread to the size of an Airstream travel trailer.
- COLOR: A shade or two darker than McDonald's french fries.
- EASE OF CAPTURE: Fair. Use a 30.06.
- LEVEL OF CHALLENGE: Fight like VC in dense canopy.
- DESIRABILITY: Fish equivalent of a '74 AMC Gremlin.
- EDIBILITY: The Surgeon General has determined that carp eating is hazardous to your health.

The Largemouth Bass

A more highly evolved sunfish with a mouth the size of a Volkswagen trunk. Highly aggressive, largemouth bass would kill you if they could figure out how to do it; for now, they have to settle for making you spend $22,500 plus finance charges on a Ranger bass boat.

Largemouth bass live everywhere that you can't throw your lure; some bass set up condos in overhanging brush and lie in wait for you to hang up a five-buck crankbait. Bigmouths also like lily pads, which account for more lost lures per square yard than any other single obstruction. Largemouth bass have become extremely finicky in recent years because of lucrative endorsement contracts with cable networks.

- NICKNAMES: Hawg; Bucketmouth; Bubba.
- SIZE: Hand-sized to the size of a gunnysack full of bricks.
- COLOR: Camouflage.
- EASE OF CAPTURE: Not as easy as certain blow dried, blond, beer-bellied TV fishing show hosts would have you believe.
- LEVEL OF CHALLENGE: Like the Red Army in a corner.
- DESIRABILITY: Highly desirable, inexplicably.
- EDIBILITY: Fried heavily, they taste like mushy onion rings.

The Smallmouth Bass

The smallmouth bass plays the Beav to the Largemouth's Wally. Smallmouths get little media attention — there are no smallmouth bass boats — but they are shockingly contentious and scare the bejeezus out of you when they're hooked. Smallmouths seem to enjoy hanging around rockpiles and viciously defend their mineral rights when a weird little plastic lure blunders into their territory. Smallmouths are fast and hardy and thrive in fairly cold water. Smallmouths are what largemouths would be if they got a little exercise.

- SIZE: They all seem to weigh two pounds. Go figure.
- COLOR: Earth tone.
- EASE OF CAPTURE: Some days you can't beat them off with a stick.
- LEVEL OF CHALLENGE: Will dislocate your shoulder.
- DESIRABILITY: Desirable, assuming they haven't been sitting uncleaned in your trunk for two days.
- EDIBILITY: Better than okra.

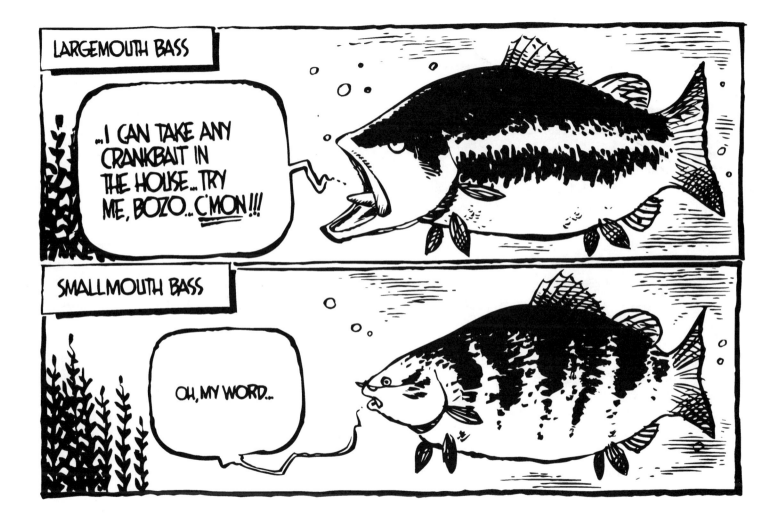

The Walleye

The walleye is the state fish of Minnesota. If you walk into a bar in Brainerd, Minnesota, it is likely that the walleye will be mentioned about every sixth word.

"So dat walleye hit my Lindy Rig and so."

"Oh, yeah? We had walleye for supper last night."

"Is that right, eh? My daughter married a walleye."

"Oh, yeah? My mother was a walleye."

"I hear they're gonna run a walleye for Governor next year."

Walleye, walleye, walleye. What is it about the walleye that inspires such passion in Minnesota and the rest of the Midwest? Sheer boredom, perhaps, but I think it's the eyes. The walleye has the creepiest, most mesmerizing, catlike stare that I have ever seen on anyone, including insurance salesmen. Walleyes just kind of hang in the water, waiting for the next leech to drift by; when they nail your rig, you feel like you've snagged an 18-wheeler going downhill. Then they suddenly slip into a coma and float to the surface. And stare at you.

- SIZE: Half are the size of bananas. The other half are the size of baseball bats.
- COLOR: Bruised bananas.
- EASE OF CAPTURE: Pretty easy, if you don't mind being stared at.
- LEVEL OF CHALLENGE: Like a thresher shark for 10 seconds, then like a deflated beachball until you get them in the boat.
- DESIRABILITY: Very desirable, in Minnesota. Of course, Fritz Mondale was desirable in Minnesota, too.
- EDIBILITY: Walleye bones are the number one killer of 63-year-old guys named Ole.

The Northern Pike

It sounds like a road to Alaska, but the northern pike is really an alligator with very short legs. Truly terrifying to behold, the northern pike — or simply "northern" to people who smell like fish all the time — is a floating repository of teeth, a meal ticket for doctors who do hand surgery, and a good way to experience a very large treble hook under your fingernail. Northerns cruise lakes in search of food: they'll eat fish, but they also enjoy 14-foot Alumacrafts with medium-sized outboards. They'll even eat baby ducks.

Only a monster eats baby ducks.

- SIZE: It's bigger than both of us.
- COLOR: Alligator colored, with splotches.
- EASE OF CAPTURE: You really don t want to catch one. They'll tear your index finger off, just for laughs. You think I'm kidding. They're meaner than Nazi war criminals.
- LEVEL OF CHALLENGE: Like trying to reel in Manhattan with your drag set on "one."
- DESIRABILITY: Only to make handbags and shoes out of.
- EDIBILITY: Eat them only for revenge.

The Muskellunge

Never, ever say "muskellunge." It's a muskie. I should have said that in the title to this piece, but publishing has its formalities. You only see "muskellunge" used in pretentious think pieces about fishing, the ones with all the graphs in the overly technical fishing magazines that read like the Bulletin of Atomic Scientists.

The muskie — no relation to former Senator Ed Muskie, who was somewhat fishy in appearance nonetheless — is the F-14 Tomcat of fish. No, it's the A-6 Intruder of fish. Or maybe the F-4 Phantom of fish. *(Editor: Fighter plane analogies can stop here.)* Anyway, it's the big, fast airplane of fish.

The muskie is the trophy fish in the Midwest. It has northern pike for meals; just pops the miserable creatures into its Hollywood Bowl-sized mouth like anchovies. Fishing for the muskie requires a firm financial commitment from the Sultan of Brunei; one muskie plug (must be one and a half feet long or longer) can cost ten bucks and you may inadvertently catch a couple of water-skiers. Not that nailing a couple of water-skiers would be a bad thing.

- SIZE: Frequently mistaken for an Airstream trailer.
- COLOR: Silvery green. Greenish silver. Something like that.
- EASE OF CAPTURE: One muskie is caught every six years in Wisconsin. It is then hung in the rotunda of the state capitol in Madison, where it is worshiped until it gets too ripe. Then people talk about it like it's the Fatima Letter.
- LEVEL OF CHALLENGE: Can be reeled in under a special suspension of the laws of physics.
- DESIRABILITY: Never catch anything that could theoretically eat you.
- EDIBILITY: Bake at 375 degrees. Cover. Add lemon and seasoning. Serves 875,000.

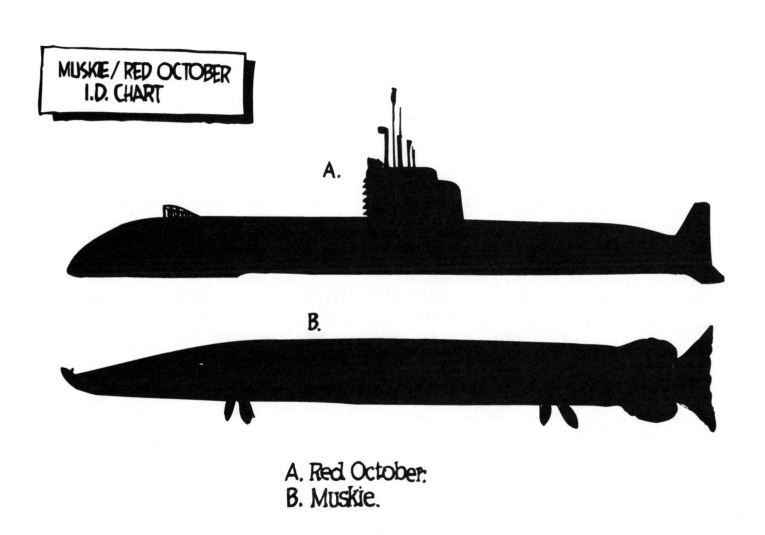

Spare The Rod, Spool The Reel

Open-Faced Spinning Reel

The most popular incarnation of all reels. It was invented in the 1940s by a guy who had thrown his seven previous baitcasting reels into the lake in fits of rage. With each passing model year, the spinning reel gets more and more complicated-looking; some marketing brainiac thought they should look like Nikons, and now they all have little numbers on them that no one ever looks at.

- ADVANTAGES OF OPEN-FACED SPINNING REEL: Looks like a camera.
- DISADVANTAGES OF OPEN-FACED SPINNING REEL: If line is overloaded on the spool, it will cascade onto the floor of the boat in intractable Slinkyesque loops. Certain models have an extremely annoying tendency to have the line get sucked under the spool and wrapped around the various gears underneath; this is more complicated to unravel than the causes of World War I.

Sometimes unlucky fishermen find themselves fighting a large fish one minute, and then staring at a broken bail the next as the fish in question strips out 750 feet of line per second. In well-meaning but inane liquor ads, would-be Madison Avenue fishermen are usually shown holding these reels pointing up instead of pointing down. This is always good for a laugh.

Closed-Face Spinning Reel

Also known as the push-button spinning reel. It operates on the same general principle as an open-faced spinning reel, except when the line gets all balled up, you can't see what happened. Some manufacturers have designed their reels so that they are virtually impossible to take apart; they figure you'll get so frustrated trying to repair them, you'll just say "screw this noise" and buy a new one. I've only done this about eight times. So I guess they're right. Damn.

- ADVANTAGES OF CLOSED-FACED SPINNING REEL: Cheap.
- DISADVANTAGES OF CLOSED-FACED SPINNING REEL: A Major Reel Manufacturer That Begins with Z makes reels with Snoopy — ® © ™ etc. — drawn on the cover of the reel. Give me a break. I mean, Good Grief.

There is also the unspoken, but nonetheless very real, assumption that if you are spotted using a closed-faced reel, you may not be a serious fisherman. It's hard to believe that fishermen, who trim their nails every Christmas and have large regions of their physique unexplored by soap, could be snobs, but there it is.

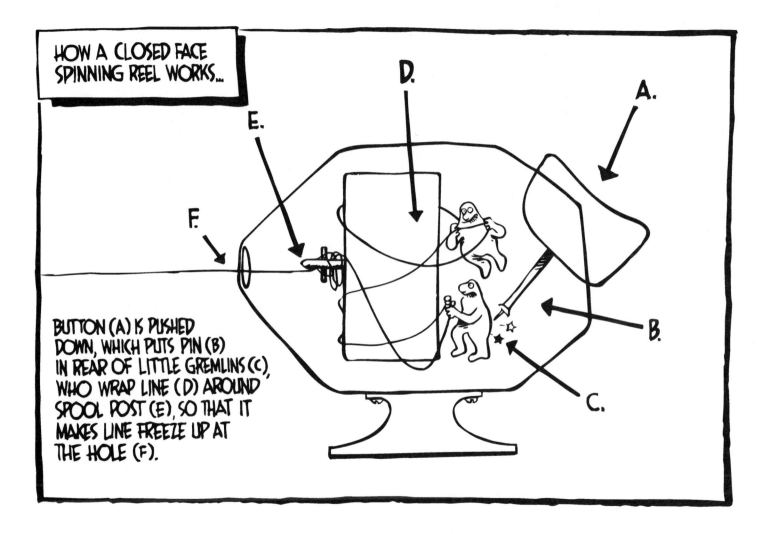

Bait-casting Reel

Theologians argue about the existence of hell. Throw some theologians together and have them attempt to learn how to cast a bait-casting reel, and you'll have your answer in short order. Not only is this miserable piece of machinery sent from Beelzebub himself, it wastes line because of Gordian Knot-sized birds' nests. The silly invention is so backward it's almost as if it was designed by NASA space shuttle engineers tripping on blotter acid and sloe gin fizzes.

- ADVANTAGES OF BAITCASTING REEL: Can be thrown into the water in frustration fairly easily due to its hand-sized design.
- DISADVANTAGES OF BAIT-CASTING REEL: Seventeenth-century technology makes it useless, even with so-called anti-backlash devices foisted off on unsuspecting rube anglers with deep pockets and shallow minds. May cause sudden death in impatient anglers with short tempers and existing heart conditions. Defies all known laws of physics.

Hot Rods

Nowhere are fishermen more completely at the mercy of the tackle industry than when they're buying a fishing rod. There used to be three types of rods: steel, bamboo and glass. The Big Three: reliable, easy to choose from, available in ugly colors, like the models from Ford, Chevy and Chrysler. Now the sharp pencil boys from the space program and marketing whiz kids have made it impossible to figure out what kind of rod to buy. Graphite? Boron? Platinum? Uranium? What is graphite, anyway? Why is it so expensive? Can it be made into jewelry? What is boron? Didn't Ronald Reagan used to sell 20 Mule Team Boron?

And then they started messing around with the ferrules. What the hell difference does it make whether the ferrules are ceramic or metal? The world's record largemouth bass was probably caught with some crappy old metal rod with metal guides. All the boron and graphite and ceramic ferrules in the world haven't produced the record-breaking bass yet. Why not? Riddle me that, Bassman. I mean, Batman.

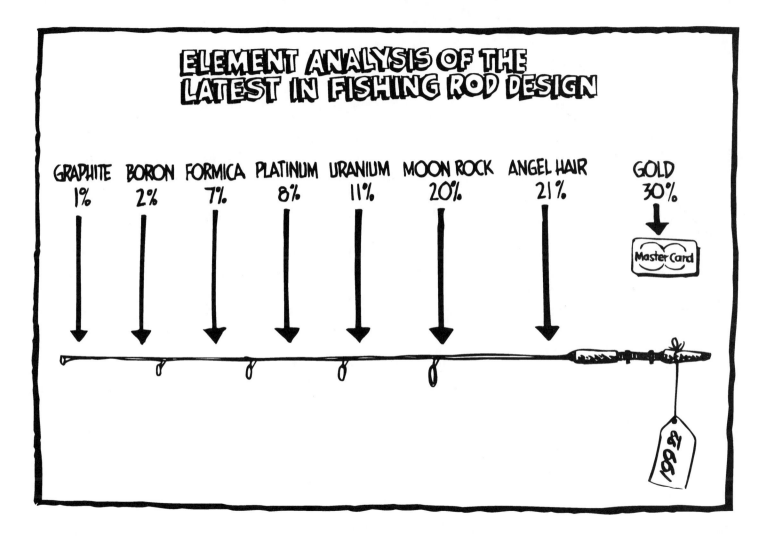

Tackle Boxes

Tackle boxes can be divided into two types: those that have trays that are melted by plastic worms, and those that don't. It's that simple. A tackle box speaks volumes about a fisherman's personality. Does the fisherman have a box wherein there is only one lure — neatly stowed, hooks honed, properly dried off — per compartment? Or is he the type of fisherman who just kind of tosses the lure into the box and hopes it lands in a tray? Whom would you rather go fishing with, Felix Unger or Oscar Madison?

Some tackle boxes are so large that they separate your shoulder at the rotator cuff, which may put a crimp in your casting technique. Avoid any tackle box that advertises a spare compartment for an outboard motor. Opening one of these behemoths is like opening Pandora's Box; curses of a thousand years are visited upon you, not to mention a full spectrographic assortment of every single permutation of fishing lure invented since the death of Izaak Walton.

Small tackle boxes, however, are worse. There's only enough room for a split shot and a broken treble hook. Having an inadequate tackle box is like going into a drug store and asking for the smallest-sized rubber; it sends the message that you're not serious.

A nasty occurrence is when your tackle box tips over with the lid closed. Open it, and you'll discover a chain of lures 60 feet long with interlocking treble hooks. The worst thing that can happen to you is to quickly pick up your tackle box with an unlocked latch. Then the entire contents explode onto the dock, and you have to spend the next two hours picking up Hula Poppers.

How the Fishing Industrial Complex Names Lures

Fishing lures are named by people who used to work for advertising agencies that had baby product accounts. All lures are named in a childish, cutely misspelled, phonetic manner that's irritating to those who have successfully completed third grade. A lot of lures have names like Snag-N-Buddy, BassBusterHawg Frawg, Li'l Skittlin' Scud-O-Rama.

Or they have overly militaristic names like Ground Zero Vapo-rizing Kill Ray-She-Oh Bass Body Kount. Some lures have vaguely sexual names like Teezin' Throbb-N Flesh Pot Muskie Hot 'N' Nasty Snatcher.

Lures to be avoided:

- Lures that claim to smell like something, like "Walleye Walloper with Hot Beef Stew Aroma."
- Lures that have LED digital readouts.
- Lures that play fish-attracting jingles.
- Lures that look like supporting players in the movie *Aliens*.
- Lures that have treble hooks with a CIA-Approved Special Shellfish Toxin on the barbs.
- Lures that require batteries or extension cords.
- Lures that have small plastic explosive charges.
- Lures that have colors that can only be appreciated under black light.
- Lures that look like they could eat your dog and enjoy it.

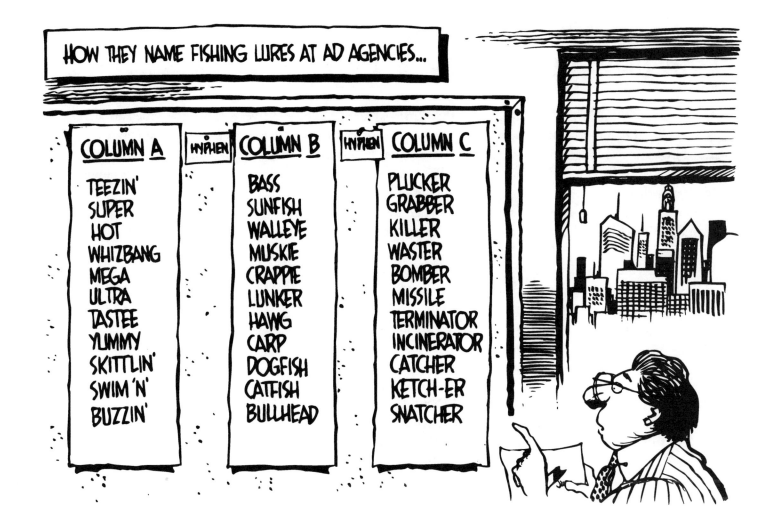

Baited Breath

Live bait is effective, probably more so than artificial lures, but over the years it has developed an unsavory reputation. Back in ancient times — say, the pre-color Loran depthfinder era — everybody used live bait and caught 89 jillion fish that we now see in photographs. You know the photo; it was taken in the 1920s, and a guy with six teeth is standing next to a rack that has 83 northern pike over 20 pounds that were caught in one afternoon with a cane pole and grasshoppers.

Nowadays, of course, we must strive for the High-Tech Fish Acquisition Solution, and that involves bells, whistles, microchips and chartreuse rubber things that look like radioactive squids.

ADVANTAGES OF THE WORM AS LIVE BAIT:
- Doesn't have a cute alliterative name
- No built-in treble hooks that dig into your palm
- Not produced in colors only found on the planet Jupiter
- Free, if you think about digging it up the night before your trip
- Probably digestible if you accidentally eat it

DISADVANTAGES OF THE WORM AS LIVE BAIT:
- Tends to make an aromatic fashion statement about you
- Squirms uncomfortably as you pass large hooks through its central nervous system
- Costs 2 bucks per dozen, at a markup of 156,000 percent
- Can escape if unattended, unlike a plastic worm

Boats, Bass and Going to Extremes

Bass Boats

In the beginning, God created the canoe. Well, maybe God didn't create the canoe, but some one with a supernatural inner ear must have. The fact is, canoes are virtually impossible to fish from, unless you're under two feet tall.

Certain purist fishermen — the guys with the fruity-smelling pipes who look like L. L. Bean catalog stuntmen — insist that canoes are the only craft that are aesthetically pleasing enough to fish from. Probably true, but sepia 1937 *Field & Stream* covers be damned; Bubba and Junior have got to catch fish and they can't do it in a simple craft like a canoe, or the pathetically underequipped rowboat. No, they've got to have a bass boat.

Bass boats are frightening-looking machines; they look as if they had been designed as some sort of venal high-tech search-and-destroy patrol boat. On the water, the hull barely visible, two or three pedestal seats balance voluptuous good ol' boys in fluorescent jumpsuits with more patches on them than Eisenhower had. Mounted on the stern is an engine that was swiped from the Talladega 500. And just what's on board these PT boats for guys who smell like eel slime? Well, you got your:

- Fully aerated, Klimate Kontrolled, Fish Longevity Isolation Tank/Livewell, filled with nice cold Schmidts (The Sport Pack, of course, with the muskie on it).
- Foot Controlled Electric Trolling Motor that can take your fingers off faster than you can say, "Keep that prop in the water, Bill."
- Graph Depth Finder that can pick up HBO and Cinemax, in addition to tracking incoming ICBMs.
- Kustom Kut Float-Rite Krushed Velour Blue Metal Flake Seats, with Magic Fingers.
- Fully Operational Fish-N-Kockpit, with Brightly Illuminated LED Readout, Very-Nearly-Like Top Gun Kontrol Konsole.

Bass Tournaments

While bass fishing is supposed to be a restful, contemplative pursuit like, say, drag racing, there are always those Type A personalities who have to introduce the element of competition. A little friendly BS about the sizes and weights of fish has always been considered derigueur, but now an insidious plague of turning fishing into a network TV game show is running unchecked throughout the nation.

Bass tournaments feature lots of massively overweight men named Hoot chasing around tranquil lakes in their bass boats with 16 gears, covering the water with surgical precision in hopes of tying into a bass that weighs more than they do. Here are the rules of a recent bass tournament:

CONTESTANTS: Please read the following guidelines for the Third Annual Bubba "Hoot" Bilbo/Shearson Lehman Memorial Bassin' Assassin Invitational.

1. Your attorney must remain at dockside. You may contact him by fax if you have a legal question while you are on the water.
2. Stuffing your largest bass with non-aquatic food such as Goo Goo Clusters and Mallomars to enhance weight is strictly forbidden.
3. All bass will be genetically fingerprinted at dockside and sent to the National Institute of Health in Bethesda, Maryland, for authentication.
4. If you are in doubt about weapons usage against your opponents, please contact the dock for caliber restrictions.
5. Lures that have more than 11 (eleven) treble hooks are expressly forbidden.
6. Bass that have been obviously tampered with, or surgically altered, or carp that have been painted to resemble bass will be confiscated and used on TV fishing shows.
7. Talking bass are worth 5 (five) bonus points.
8. Depth charges, torpedoes, cruise missiles, and other concussive fishing enhancement and procurement devices must be registered with the Joint Chiefs of Staff and the dock.

Toy Boat, Toy Boat, Toy Boat

There are, of course, different types of fishing boats besides the bass boat. A perennial favorite is the so-called "cartopper" aluminum fishing boat. These boats can be easily put on top of your car in a matter of hours with surprisingly little long-term damage to your spine and knuckles.

THE ALUMINUM CARTOPPER, SUMMER: You'll bake like the Pillsbury Doughboy in 20 minutes. Acts as a convex mirror and focuses all of the sun's nuclear fury on your nose and then proceeds to burn you beyond recognition. If you survive this onslaught, then you can look forward to burning your fingers and hands on the gunwales all day.

THE ALUMINUM CARTOPPER, FALL: Has the refrigerative qualities of freon. Wet skin may fuse to aluminum surface, form a bond, and have to be filleted off with your Normark fishing knife.

ADVANTAGES OF THE ALUMINUM CAR TOPPER:
• Can blind other fishermen with the sun's rays, eliminating competition.
• Can be dropped from a height of 600 feet without popping a rivet.
• If filled with ice, can be used as a beer cooler at a party.

DISADVANTAGES OF THE ALUMINUM CAR TOPPER:
• Looks stupid if you paint a name on the side.
• Tends to exaggerate any noise; a dropped split shot sounds like a twelve-gauge riot gun at three feet.
• In rough weather, makes you feel like you just stepped from the promenade deck of the Titanic.

The Norwegian Walleye Sled

This craft is the dream boat of the Norwegian who wants to blow a lot of money on a fishing boat, but wants the boat to look kind of shabby so the wife doesn't think he's up to no good. The Norwegian Walleye Sled is a 16- to 18-foot aluminum monster that is a triumph of function over form. Only the barest of fishing essentials are on board; it's kind of like being in solitary confinement with walleye fishing as your only diversion.

The Norwegian Walleye Sled's floor tends to accumulate garbage that, over the years, never seems to get picked up. On the bottom of the boat you'll find Eagle Claw hook packages from the 1950s; an assembled multitude of thousands of split shot that rolls around on the aluminum surface when the boat moves even slightly, loudly heralding your arrival to fish before you drop anchor; and mummified nightcrawlers that are older than Ramses II.

Come to think of it, Ramses II might make pretty good walleye bait.

Zen and the Art of Outboard Motor Maintenance

Outboard motors are an integral part of the fishing experience. They provide that redolent petroleum/dead dinosaur smell that clings to the true fisherman for days after the trip, an olfactory reminder even more pungent than leech juice.

You see a lot of outboard motors on the lake, and everybody else's seem to start up on the first pull. Attempting to get that nasty little five horse gizmo humming while you're two miles from shore, a huge thunderboomer building up to gale force and heading your way is one of life's ways of telling you to take up golf. Grown men weeping openly over an internal combustion engine is nature's most pathetic sight, next to watching someone learn to fly cast.

To start the outboard, you must do the following:

- GRASP the cord handle in your right hand.
- PULL back violently, as if a Gaboon Viper were hanging from your index finger.
- SEPARATE your shoulder from its cartilaginous moorings because the engine is frozen stiff.
- SCREAM in agony as the pain message reaches your cerebral cortex.
- INVOKE Anglo-Saxon expressions and scatological nomenclature.
- PULL AGAIN, and watch helplessly as the cord whips you in the face as it detaches itself neatly from the starter.
- SWAB the whip mark from your face with iodine or Uncle Josh's Pork Rind fluid.
- CALL 911.

Ice Station Zebco

Ice fishing isn't really a sport, or a pursuit, or even a mental illness. It's a form of discipline. In fact, it's in Wisconsin's statutes as their maximum criminal punishment. Fishing, even when it's 72 degrees and sunny, requires quite a bit of effort and planning. Ice fishing requires, even before you begin, that you cut a hole in the ice with either an ice pick or an ice auger, which resembles a dentist's fondest sadomasochistic dream. After a bracing aerobic drilling session, which can last an eternity, particularly if you're cutting a hole big enough for your boat, you're ready to begin.

You can fish out in the open, huddled over your hole, watching the water slowly develop a glaze and then freeze over entirely with your hapless bobber held hostage. Of course, some wise guy from Duluth has retired to the Lesser Antilles (no ice fishing there) on the earnings from his ice hole ice skimmer, which is a kind of glorified spaghetti strainer you will use every three minutes. These things really exist, I swear.

You have a one in three chance of surviving your ice fishing trip; your odds for survival are further reduced if you build a huge bonfire on the ice and stand real close to it.

The less hardy ice fisherman will drive his '72 Buick Skylark right onto the ice, drill a hole next to the driver's door while his heater blasts away, and hang his pole — two feet long — right out the window. The drawbacks to this method include the very real possibility — this happens every year in Minnesota and Wisconsin — that an ice floe will break off with the poor sap and his clunker drifting slowly out to sea, at the mercy of the National Guard to airlift him to safety minus the death car, which then is consigned to Davy Jones' locker when the ice melts.

But the real sybarite will have his own ice house, which is configured exactly like an outhouse, and fish right through the floor. Imagine the fun that is! Lazy ice fishermen who wait until the last minute to get their ice house off the lake wind up with an underwater condo.

Smile, You're on Catfish Camera

Television Fishing Shows

Many people are first exposed to fishing courtesy of the cathode ray tube. While it's not exactly the next best thing to being there, it does provide a certain vicarious thrill and you don't have to expose yourself to any elements not found in your refrigerator. Unfortunately, television fishing programs are no more realistic than Willard Scott's hairline.

Fishing programs fall into three categories. The first show is an overly technical, jargon laden scientific presentation that requires a master's in fisheries management and a minor in electrical engineering to understand. Unfortunately, it's usually hosted by a guy from central Louisiana who speaks some half-French, half-English dialect spoken only by swamp dwellers with unusually acute hearing. So any practical information presented is lost in the translation. Perhaps English subtitles are the answer.

The second type of fishing show is presented as a boring 1950s home movie/travelogue format with the production values of an eighth grade Soviet audiovisual class. The host speaks in a vaguely patronizing monotone about the various glories of the exotic locale he is in and you, poor sap, are not. Very little actual fishing is done, but there are lots of factoids about the average annual rainfall and gauzy panoramic shots of the host not catching anything.

The third fishing show is the "Hey Dude, Let's Party!" good ol' boy program that includes lots of shots of the immense host's lacquered blond hair, and the oft-repeated phrase, "Whooooooo-eeee!" Quick cuts of the host's nuclear-powered bass boat turning lily pads into Caesar salad and frequent brand-name references are the dead giveaways.

Fishing the Global Village

Let's take a quick, *Fishing Bass-Ackwards* look at a recent sampling of the cable listings for TV fishing shows:

(13) (FISHNET) KICKIN' BASS with "Scooter" Analvent. Join Scooter as he heads into Cambodia's rice paddies in his De-Ranger Bass Boat and kicks largemouth bass and commie ass. Scooter is joined by Cambodian bass guide Bhat Ton Rouge, who has a wider command of English than the Ol' Scootman. The "Mister Mister Twisted Sister Bassin' Blisterer" lure will be field-tested in a monsoon and under light to moderate small arms fire.

(16) (PBS) THE AIRBORNE ANGLER. The Airborne Angler travels this week to the Tigris and the Euphrates to jig for walleyes as the ancient Egyptians did 3,000 years ago. Then we travel to the Soviet Union's world-famous Chernobyl radioactive sloughs for crappie fishing with Mikhail Gorbachev, and then on to the North Pole for ice fishing through the ice cap with the grandchildren of Admiral Peary. Made possible by a grant from the John T. and Catherine D. MacArthur Foundation, the Chubb Group of Insurance Companies, and Al's House O'Minnows Tackle Shop.

(24) (FIN-SPN) THE PHYSICS OF FISHING 201 with Dr. Normark Rapala. Dr. Rapala demonstrates leech fishing while using whale noises to call in unsuspecting walleyes, and tests the tensile strength of crappie lips with the aid of the space shuttle *Atlantis* crew. With charts, graphs, tables, quadratic polynomials, Boolean algebra, quantum mechanics, space-based laser technology, Ground Wave Electronics Networks, free-radicals, rogue genes, and really, really big numbers. Companion workbook available at small arrogant private Eastern college bookstores. Four credits. M-Th-F.

The Amazing Differences Between a TV Fishing Show and Donahue

TV FISHING SHOW	DONAHUE
No sensitive male host, as a rule	So sensitive you want to gag
Shot on a lake or stream	Shot in a New York studio
People sitting around talking about crankbaits	People sitting around talking about cross dressing
Lots of super fishing	Lots of superficial
Great hairstyle on host	So-so hairstyle on host
Really fast boats	Really fast mouths
Fish eggs	Frozen embryos
Plastic worms	Plastic guests
Useful information about bass	Useless information about bastards
Overalls with fish guts on them	$1,500 suits with spilled guts on them
Surface lures	Surface tensions
Men talking with other men about panfish	Men talking with other men about pansexuals

The Something Fishy Fishing Catalog

Carp and Catfish "Clean" Isolation Suit

Is there anything worse than actually touching a carp or a catfish? Probably not — that's why scientists at the Rocky Flats nuclear weapons plant in Denver developed this isolation suit for handling carp and catfish, the only two fish known to cause cancer in laboratory animals. Just slip on the handsome lead/copper lined garment, flip down the visor, and you're ready to handle carp and catfish up to 40 pounds!
$450.
Specify S-M-L-XL.
Color: Bright Yellow.

Bass Boas

When they catch the world's record bass someday, do you think it'll be on some wimpy little lure like a shad or a plastic worm? Heck no. It'll be on a Bass Boa — the World's Longest Lure! The Bass Boa is a 30-foot long Boa Constrictor, specially imported from the Amazon, and man, does it catch big bass! But be careful — the Bass Boa could take you out in one gulp!

$45/doz.

Colors: Grape, Chartreuse, Cinnamon, Day-Glo Orange.

12-Gauge Bassblaster Surface Plug

The Big One won't get away with this lure! When Mr. Bucketmouth nails this topwater plug, he'll be in for a big surprise when he accidentally hits the primer on this ingenious shotgun shell/bait.

$4.95.
Colors: Red, Green, Blue, Camouflage, Chartreuse.

"Cap'n Nemo" Walleye Sub

Tired of chasing walleyes all over tarnation without knowing just exactly where they are? Our designers — former E-5s on the USS Ohio nuclear submarine —have solved the walleye location problem for all time with this 340-foot U-boat. Imagine the hours of fishing enjoyment as you take walleye after walleye with the handy cruise missiles.

$6,000,000,000.00
FOB Groton, CT.
Color: Black.

Lake Drain

How many times have you said, "I wish I could drain the lake to see where the Big Ones live?" Now you can with the Lake Drain. A little known hydrological fact is that every lake, in fact, does have a drain. The Lake Drain helps you find it and then, utilizing space-age geological drilling techniques, sucks the water out into sparsely populated low-lying areas. Millions of fish will be yours for the taking. Good luck!

$79.95.

Color: Chrome with red spigot.

Kute Flote-Rite "Muskie-Lunge" Kitten And Puppy Harness

Everyone knows that muskies are the most vicious behemoths in the lake, and that they've even been known to hit baby ducks on the surface, but why stop there? The Kitten and Puppy Harness holds either cute li'l critter on the surface for hours, and ingeniously frees the pets when nasty ol' Mr. Muskie makes his move. Includes Kitten and Puppy Life Vest.

$15.95.

Color: Brown.

The Tackle Boat

Sometimes it seems like you're carrying 800 pounds of tackle boxes around with you, and you want relief —fast! That's where the Tackle Boat comes in. No more schlepping huge ABS plastic behemoths around filled with one color of plastic worm ... the tackle boat is a floating tackle box with 8,900 — count 'em! — individual tackle trays waiting to be filled with your junk.

$5,600.00.

Colors: Green, Tan, Amber.

Motor not included.

Silent Partner Fishing Buddy

If you're tired of that overly chatty boat companion, you'll love the Silent Partner Fishing Buddy. Instead of endless prattle about the weather, fish stories from the 1970s, and inane advice, the Silent Partner Fishing Buddy keeps you company without stupid asides and dopey rejoinders. The Silent Partner is inflatable and is also a U.S. Coast Guard Approved Personal Flotation Device, which is more helpful than your real-life boatmate when your boat is sinking.

$29.95.

Colors: Caucasian, Black, Asian.

(Please specify expression: Happy, Sad, Indifferent.)

Bass Boat Animated Signal Scoreboard

When you're out on the lake during a bass tournament, you don't want to be using confusing hand signals and arm waving to communicate with your opponents — you need the Bass Boat Animated Signal Scoreboard. This bow-mounted scoreboard is just like the one at the Kingdome in Seattle. Displays number of fish caught, weight, length, water temperature, and the size of the tournament purse. It also has 25 pre-set messages, such as "WATCH YOUR WAKE, SCUMBAG," "YOU CALL THAT A BASS?" "EAT PLASTIC WORMS AND DIE" and "YOUR DEPTH FINDER SIGNAL IS INTERFERING WITH MY ELECTRIC MOTOR BATTERY, BUDDY."

$34,000.

Color: Black with white letters.

Johnz Hopkinz Gentle
Sturgeon Surgeon Hook Disgorger

Let's face it, removing hooks from fish is distasteful and messy. But with the Gentle Sturgeon Surgeon Hook Disgorger, you can operate right on your boat! And that's with a 94 percent survival rate — better than Dr. Michael DeBakey! The Gentle Sturgeon Surgeon Hook Disgorger comes with anesthesia, an operating table, scrubs, a full set of scalpels, retractors, and hemostats, and a heart-gill machine. Fun ... and humane!

$670.00 a day.

(Medicare available. Malpractice insurance may not be available in all states.)

Spray-Blond TV Fishing Show Host Hair Color

Have you ever noticed that all TV fishing show hosts have the same electric phosphorescent orange/blond hair as most pro golfers? That's no accident; their hair color is mandated by the National Association of TV Fishing Show Hosts. Now you, too, can have this unnaturally iridescent color on your hair. Studies show that people with this hair color catch 60 percent more fish, too ... so buy a can today!

$5.95.

Color: Weird orangy blond only.

Absolutely Useless Fishing Hints

What I've Learned About Fishing, 1960-1995

1960 — Nothing.

1961 — Nothing.

1962 — Nothing.

1963 — Have some dim awareness of what it is.

1964 — Something my dad does to get out of the house.

1965 — Sunfish are suicidal.

1966 — Without much trouble at all, a kid's Zebco fishing outfit can cast up to the telephone wires.

1967 — Learned that even a bass will occasionally stoop to eating worms on a bobber.

1968 — Attempts to fish in a biologically dead creek prove fruitless.

1969 — Receive a Sears fishing rod and reel for birthday present; learn a sharp lesson three years later about Sears' quality control.

1970 — Learn how to troll for trout in Utah with deep-sea fishing rigs. Effective, but tiring.

1971 — Catch numerous suckers on doughballs in Pennsylvania creek. Learned even suckers can be finicky, even though they're ugly.

1972 — Cryogenically storing bass in our basement freezer for display purposes until 1975 is frowned upon by my mother.

1972 — The aforementioned Sears reel, which saw little action until 1972, explodes when a 20-pound northern seizes a Dardevle. No one is injured, particularly the northern, which escapes when I attempt to strip the line in hand over hand. Learn that six-pound test is a marketing lie.

1973 — Ice fishing is the equivalent of playing chess with yourself.

1973 — Found that it is possible to catch 5,000 sunfish in one afternoon, if you're motivated to do so.

1974 — Learned that a tremendous whip cracking noise can be made with a fly rod.

1974 — I catch a four-pound bass on a Little Cleo. Later discover Little Cleo isn't a bass lure.

1975 — Revelation One: large northern pike can be hooked on six weight fly rod and a size 12 Red Ibis. Revelation Two: large northern pike cannot be landed on said outfit.

1976 — Learn that Governor Jimmy Carter has a fish pond at his farm in Plains, Georgia — and drains it to get the fish out. Hmmm. A portent.

1977 — Begin fly fishing for brown trout in Wisconsin. Discover that three full-time jobs are needed to finance habit.

1978 — Catch 14-inch brown on nymph and run upstream to tell friend. En route to friend, run into 17-old kid with 21-inch brown caught on Zebco with worm. I learn something.

1979 — Drive 1,000 miles to Florida and catch one eight-inch bass in six days of fishing. I learn something else.

1980 — Catch nothing.

1981 — Buy $5,000 used bass boat and catch nothing on it. I learn something yet again.

1982 — I get married and fish a lot less than I used to, coincidentally.

1983 — I move to Oregon in search of fish. Begin to think fish are secretly running my life.

1984 — I learn Walter Mondale can't parlay his walleye fishing ability into carrying the Midwest.

1985 — Learn that muskies will only strike when you have just finished a long diatribe about how slow the fishing is.

1986 — Learn how to catch 25 large browns in small stream and think I'm Theodore Gordon.

1987 — Catch no browns in same stream at exact same time of year using exactly same equipment and fly pattern.

1988 — Learn how to hook large rainbow in river and stick rod underwater to avoid detection by passing pickup trucks.

1989 — Pay $600 for three-day trip to fishing camp and catch nothing substantial until last morning. Learn yet again.

1995 — Discover that I write about fishing all the time and never actually fish.

The State of Fishing

Many beginning fishermen want to know what kind of fishing is available near them. Just for those anglers, provided below is a handy state-by-state guide to the most popular fish and fishing methods in each state.

ALABAMA — Bass. Use lots of deep fried baits and chum with Budweiser.
ALASKA — Salmon, halibut. Prepare to have your shoulder separated as you spend relaxing days reeling in 200-pound halibut and 75-pound salmon.
ARIZONA — Any fish here have evolved into scorpions.
ARKANSAS — Bass, so they claim. You have to drive to Texarkana, Texas to get beer, which is a drawback.
CALIFORNIA — Trout, bass, ocean fishing. Sushi is a good bet for bait.
COLORADO — Trout. Colorado fishermen are generally snobs, even though they use bobbers — so-called "strike detectors" — on their frighteningly expensive fly rods.
CONNECTICUT — There are no fish in Connecticut. Too close to New York.
DELAWARE — Soft-shelled crabs. Use anti-tank weapons for quick if messy results.
FLORIDA — Bass, alligators. Use college sophomores at Daytona Beach for bait.
GEORGIA — Bass, suckers. Don't fish on Jimmy Carter's pond without Secret Service permission.
HAWAII — Massive, unfriendly ocean fish with teeth like Veg-o-matics. Harpoons, submarine-launched cruise missiles seem to do the trick.
IDAHO — Trout. Using live bait is a Class A misdemeanor.
ILLINOIS — Neon tetras found in aquariums. Fry up a mess of neon tetras, and you're talking good eating.
INDIANA — Carp. Use old shoes, empty milk cartons, and pork rinds.

IOWA — Flat, dull fish. Canned corn is the killer bait.

KANSAS — There are no known bodies of water in Kansas.

KENTUCKY — Bass, crappies. Use tobacco plugs and a splash of bourbon.

LOUISIANA — Bottom feeders. Mutter bigoted epithets for best results.

MAINE — All species, but order them through an L. L. Bean catalog and save yourself the trouble.

MARYLAND — Blues. They always talk about blues, but I don't think anyone really knows what the hell they are.

MASSACHUSETTS — Nothing in Boston Harbor except for dead fish, which are easy to catch once they've washed up on shore.

MICHIGAN — All fish have moved to Texas.

MINNESOTA — Land of Ten Thousand Lakes. Walleyes, Northerns. Change your name to Lars or Hjalmar to make the fish more comfortable.

MISSISSIPPI — Catfish. That's it. And why would you want to catch those?

MISSOURI — Bass, crappie, catfish. Huck Finn may have caught them all.

MONTANA — Trout. They only respond to three dollar flies.

NEBRASKA — Corn. Corn isn't a fish, so save your money.

NEVADA — Nobody fishes in Nevada.

NEW HAMPSHIRE — Heck if I know.

NEW YORK — Used condoms, medical waste. Abundant and easy to catch.

NEW JERSEY — Hardy species of fish that have adapted to swimming in water that's about 500,000 parts per million toxic crud.

NEW MEXICO — Trace of water, microbes. Microbes have an extremely soft strike.

NORTH DAKOTA — Walleyes. But it's like fishing on the surface of the moon.

NORTH CAROLINA — Snakes. Use Jesse Helms speeches to anesthetize them.

OKLAHOMA — Rand McNally left this state out of their atlas because of space restrictions, so let's continue the practice.

OHIO — Fish with fungi so virulent that only trained wildlife biologists should attempt to touch them.

OREGON — My home state. Arrogant fish who refuse to bite my lures, even though they know I'm a fishing book author.

PENNSYLVANIA — Suckers. Doughballs with .22 bullets inside should do the trick.

RHODE ISLAND — Mafioso wise guys with cement overshoes, rusty bedsprings. Neither are gamefish.

SOUTH CAROLINA — Mean-spirited ocean fish, bass. Try jelly sandwiches.

SOUTH DAKOTA — Walleyes that make you want to hide under your boat seat. Use a 36-ounce Louisville Slugger to subdue them.

TENNESSEE — These southern states kind of run together for me.

TEXAS — Big, obnoxious fish that think they're the center of the universe. Chuck roast a prime fish producer.

UTAH — Mormon trout. They won't bite if you drink coffee around them.

VERMONT — Trout about the size of your thumb nail. Size 28 flies tied on electron scanning microscopes.

VIRGINIA — Bass, sunnies, trout. Grits are a killer.

WASHINGTON — Salmon, trout. Trawlers seem to work best.

WEST VIRGINIA — Coal for bait is a concept that should be explored.

WISCONSIN — Like Minnesota, except they have 9,999 lakes, and are quite sensitive about it.

WYOMING — Trout. Won't bite unless you buy one of those straw cowboy hats.

Glossary

ACTION — Something that happens in the other boat.

BAITCASTING — A primitive method of fishing made popular during the late Middle Ages before the invention of spinning reels.

BASS — Pit bull with a dorsal fin.

BASS BOAT — A '79 Dodge Charger with an aerated livewell.

BASS HOOK — Lower frequency hook.

BASSMASTER — President Bush's self-proclaimed favorite magazine (I'll bet).

BITE — Something that happens every seven hours, on average.

CAST — Worn on leg after trying to jump between the dock and the boat.

CATCH AND RELEASE — What fruits from Back East do.

DIPNET — An insulting rejoinder, e.g., "You dipnet!"

DRAG — Process to recover fishermen who thought a peanut butter sandwich would work "just as well" as a boat drain plug.

DROP OFF — What you do when the fish aren't biting.

EXTENSION BUTT — What happens when you spend too much time sitting on boat cushions.

FIGHTING BUTT — Your attempt to lose the extension butt by diet and exercise.

FINGERLING — What's left of your finger after you accidentally grab your filet knife instead of the Rapala.

FISH SCENT — Used to be $1.98 perfume, but is sold to you as fish scent at $4.95.

FRESHWATER — Something that large polluting corporations are trying to eliminate from the planet.

GAFF — Inappropriate remark made to a fish.

HOOK BARB — Small metal protrusion designed to make it impossible to remove hook from the back of your hand or ear.

HOOK EYE — A concept too painful to discuss.

HOOK POINT — A piece of metal that breaks off on contact with a fish's mouth.

HOOK SHANK — Hook that goes into your leg.

KNOTLESS LEADER — Contradiction in terms.

FIG. A. "FISH SCENT"

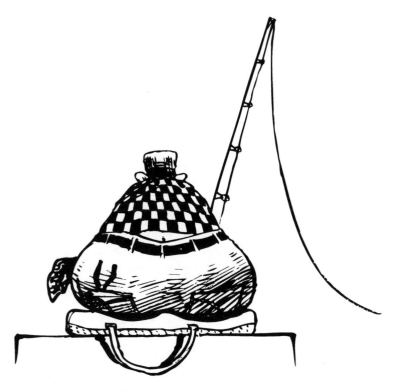

FIG. B. "EXTENSION BUTT"

LEADER — Defective monofilament sold to fishermen in short pieces.

LEECH — Fishing companion who always borrows your lures and loses them.

LINE — Defective monofilament sold to fishermen in long pieces.

MINNOW — Eight-pound muskie.

NET — Large scoop with a strange electromagnetic field that repels fish near boats.

PANFISH — This is a stupid word. I mean, as opposed to "rotisserie fish," or what?

PERCH — Small, irritating fish that forces you to constantly rebait your hook in search of real fish.

PIKE — Latin. Literally, "psychofish."

POUND TEST — The factory measured tensile strength of monofilament. Tends to be three to six pounds less than advertised in actual fishing conditions.

REEL — A line storage device that arranges monofilament around its own internal gears. Still unperfected.

REEL SEAT — Place where the reel comes off from the rod when a large fish is hooked.

SALTWATER — Where fish that can eat you in one gulp live.

SCHOOL — Where no professional bass fishermen have been since ninth grade.

SPAWN — What fishermen say when they want to get laid.

SPINNING — Fishing method that can take up to 200 yards of monofilament and put it on the floor of your boat in two seconds.

STRIKE — What a fisherman says he had when his lure snags on a stump.

TACKLE — Fancy word for little pieces of plastic and rubber with an 800 percent markup.

TIDE — Laundry detergent.

TREBLE HOOK — Higher frequency hook. See Bass Hook for lower frequency hook.

 TROLLING — Hypnotic device.

TROUT — Fish prized by Eastern Establishment Trilateral Commission Members Who Hate America And Bass.

WEEDS — Lure salad.

FIG. C. "LEECH"

FIG. D. "STRIKE"

Lists

Five Things Not to Say to a Bank Fisherman

1. "Excuse me, sir, but are you still alive?"
2. "Let me get those cobwebs for you."
3. "Your fish have turned into skeletons in this bucket."
4. "I guess you didn't hear they spilled a bunch of nuclear waste in this lake last year."
5. "That guy right next to you is just reeling 'em in, one after another."

Ten Things Not to Say to the Fish and Game Officer

1. "You sure are pudgy considering you have an outdoor job."
2. "I didn't know fishing with M-80s was unlawful, officer."
3. "Oh, for God's sake, it's not like you're a real cop or anything."
4. "Do you know Smokey the Bear?"
5. "I guess my thinking was that this is such a small state that fishing licenses weren't required."
6. "Is that your real name on that badge or a joke?"
7. "No, but I have 413 bass in my trunk."
8. "You mean boats need registrations?"
9. "Thanks for screwing up the fishing with your outboard, Clint Eastwood."
10. "Are you sure this is your jurisdiction? I'll bet it isn't."

Five Excuses Not to Use with Your Wife When You Want to Go Fishing

1. "Because you're driving me out of my mind."
2. "Because you reminded me of a walleye when we first started dating and I want to recapture that feeling."
3. "Because there's a lot of yardwork to do this weekend and I'd like to worm out of it."
4. "Because I just bought a $13,000 bass boat on our MasterCard and I want to try it out."
5. "Because Wally and Beav and Whitey and Eddie are all going, too."

Five Things Not to Say to a Guy in a Bass Boat

1. "Isn't that last year's color scheme?"
2. "How can such a little boat hold such a fat sumbitch like you-all?"
3. "I'll bet you don't keep a big, loaded revolver on board."
4. "Whoooeee! I can smell you from way over here."
5. "Is that a bass or your lure?"

Five Things Not to Say to a Tackle Shop Owner

1. "Boy, this whole fishing thing has me buffaloed. What do I need to buy?"
2. "Do you have any paisley plastic worm boxes?"
3. "Where's a good place to go fishing in the Western Hemisphere?"
4. "Two bucks for 12 little worms?"
5. "Can I have all your dead minnows for free?"

Ten Great Places to Fish for Carp

1. Primordial soup.
2. Pre-1970 Lake Erie.
3. An effluent treatment facility.
4. Standing water in your basement.
5. That little ditch in front of your house after it rains.
6. Any campground john.
7. Hanford Nuclear Reservation.
8. Your gutters.
9. A barrel of toxic waste.
10. The New York City sewer system.

Ten Lure Concepts That Never Got Off the Ground

1. Hot dogs for walleyes.
2. Infrared and ultraviolet plastic worms.
3. Lures that hum little tunes with a microchip.
4. Heavy Metal rock group endorsements of spinnerbaits.
5. Lures that actually look like something in nature.
6. Fish-shaped vitamins with tiny hooks in them.
7. The lure shaped like a ballpoint pen.
8. Lures with LED readouts that tell jokes to fish.
9. The Hand Grenade-O-Matic.
10. Subliminal tapes for fish that say, "Hit the Mister Twister ... hit the Mister Twister."

Five Surefire Ways to Catch Muskies

1. Call in Navy Carrier Task Force.
2. Float cow carcasses on surface.
3. Attempt to impersonate a female muskie in heat.
4. Jump into the water and start yelling underwater, "Muskie! Muskie! Muskie!"
5. Deck mounted harpoons.

Five Surefire Ways Not to Catch Bass

1. Spend a lot of money on your boat.
2. Let your kids play Guns 'N' Roses music to lure them in.
3. Refer to them, with an absolutely straight face, as "Ol' Bucketmouth."
4. Fly to Florida and hire a $200-a-day guide.
5. Take acid and attempt to walk on the lilypads to get closer to them.

Steelheading: Western Religion or Alien Hoax?

Has Anyone Actually Seen A Steelhead?

In the Pacific Northwest, where I happen to be at this very moment, the No. 1 gamefish is the steelhead. The fact is, the only people I have ever met who have claimed to have caught one are not exactly credible, and may even have minor criminal records. The fact is, I have never caught one. The fact is, I have never even seen one. The fact is, I don't think there are steelhead.

Consider this. The Pacific Northwest is full of people who claim to have seen D. B. Cooper, Bigfoot, and Bhagwan Shree Rajneesh's Rolls Royce mechanic, and therefore have a fairly loose grasp on reality to begin with. So when a Pacific Northwesterner tells me about his fantastic steelhead fishing, I nod graciously and at all the appropriate moments, but secretly know ing that the guy is snowing me.

Ask yourself these questions when you consider going steelhead fishing:

• Have I ever actually seen a steelhead in person?
• Would I even know what a steelhead was if I caught it?
• Why do I want to fish for something that's nothing more than a baseless rumor?

If you do go steelheading, here are some things to watch out for:

• Avoid people who tell you they can "see" the steelhead in the water. Ask them if they can see Jimmy Hoffa.

• Steelhead fishing is said to be decent only when its 33 degrees and sleeting. This makes you wonder if they're not trying to keep you away with lousy weather because there aren't really any steelhead.

• Steelhead can only be caught on "steelhead rods" and "steelhead lures." Why are they so special that they get their own equipment? Tackle manufacturer's conspiracy, or mere coincidence?

And one more question:

• Steelhead are — allegedly — really rainbow trout; so, if they exist, why the pseudonym?

The Amazing Differences Between Steelhead Fishing and Standing in a Desert with a Stick

STEELHEAD FISHING	STANDING IN DESERT WITH STICK
No fish caught	No fish caught
Water	No water
Have lots of doubts about the whole enterprise	Have lots of doubts about the whole enterprise
Freezing your ass off in the rain	Warm, dry
Slipping on slimy boulders	No slime on boulders
Never see anyone else catch steelhead	Never see anyone else catch a steelhead
Questioning of your sanity	Questioning your sanity
Disgusting salmon eggs all over your hands	Dirt, dust on your hands
Endure endless streamside prattle on how to catch steelhead	No one prattling
No bites	Scorpion bites

Meet The Fishermen

DuWayne Wayne Wayne

OCCUPATION: Carburetion Analyst

FAVORITE FISH: Largemouth Bass (pronounced Logmowf Base)

FAVORITE FISHING METHOD: Likes to use live farm animals as bait; wears heavy camouflage jumpsuit with Vietnam patches on it, even though he served in the Indiana National Guard with Dan Quayle. Has shot bass with a crossbow while hanging from overhead branches. Aromatically indistinguishable from his quarry. Covers face with burned cork, "just in case." Keeps .44 under boat cushion to finish off bass that won't go quietly.

FAVORITE LURE: Piece of fried chicken on a frog harness.

QUOTE: "Bass is the enemy. Waste them all and let God sort them out."

Odin Thor Torskssenssonssensson

OCCUPATION: "I am retired 34 years retired from the Soo Line Railroad Company and so."

FAVORITE FISH: Walleye

FAVORITE FISHING METHOD: Bobbing endlessly in the middle of a lake 20 miles across in six-foot waves because it reminds him of the fjords. Hunkers down in 18-foot Norwegian Walleye Sled, wearing seven layers of red wool union suits and a three-dollar rainsuit from K mart. Ties on huge weighted leech rig to anchor the boat in swells. Prefers to fish when the weather is rotten because "your leech jiggles around better in bad winds."

FAVORITE LURE: "I think walleyes like ugly lures so I use your Lazy Ike with your sucker minnow and your pork rind tail and your catfish-scent fish spray and an Oh Henry candy bar."

QUOTE: "This weather is nothing. In 1958, my brother got swept over the side while he was fighting a 7-pound walleye and the search planes found him two days later, treading water and trying to figure out how to land the walleye. So this is nothing."

"I don't want my name used."

OCCUPATION: Social outcast.

FAVORITE FISH: Carp.

FAVORITE FISHING METHOD: Likes to fish for carp with doughballs. Willingly hangs around sloughs and standing water that smell like a cross between an oil refinery and an outdoor biffie. Thinks carp fight hard; has formulated special doughballs scented with 10W/40 motor oil, bacon grease, and old cat litter. Throws doughballs into swamp and then watches for carp wakes heading for hook. Sets hook on carp and then actually attempts to land the fish.

FAVORITE LURE: "I like three-day-old wet garbage."

QUOTE: "I can stop fishing for carp anytime I want."

Otis Pike

OCCUPATION: Bully, sadist, junior high wrestling coach. Third Reich paraphernalia collector.
FAVORITE FISH: Northern pike.
FAVORITE FISHING METHOD: Enjoys the sheer nastiness of the northern pike and revels in provoking it. Likes to troll for hours until butt becomes numb from outboard motor vibration. Uses leaders made of brake cable; builds up biceps from reeling in lures that have 13 treble hooks. Prefers skulking around reeds and secretly hopes that fish do feel pain. Wears black leather while fishing.
FAVORITE LURE: Baseball bat painted like a minnow with grappling hooks (shark meat optional).
QUOTE: "I love the smell of northern pike in the morning."

Verne "Catfish" Catatonia

OCCUPATION: Unable to remember to look for work.

FAVORITE FISH: "Catfish, bullhead, anything on the bottom."

FAVORITE FISHING METHOD: Throws out package of moldy baloney attached to 3/0 hook. Sits on bank of river and stares at a fixed point about 75 yards in the middle distance with mouth just slightly open, permitting excess saliva to escape and dribble harmlessly on his T-shirt. Prefers not to be disturbed by fish, but will generally pick up the cane pole and mime as if a fish were actually on if people are watching.

FAVORITE LURE: "Well sir, I like the baloney, but I also like the Velveeta. I like to have the choice of either using my bait or eating it myself."

QUOTE: "I'm not here."

Hamilton Fish

OCCUPATION: Assembly line worker, serial fisherman.
FAVORITE FISH: Panfish, any kind, preferably in vast numbers.
FAVORITE FISHING METHOD: Likes to row out into the middle of a small lake in a jonboat and jerk in a couple thousand sunnies. Quits fishing when the dead sunnies reach his knees or when the boat sinks, whichever comes first. Hauls the sunnies back to shore, where he spends the next nine hours scraping scales.
   Constantly trying to figure new ways to catch sunnies; is currently negotiating with the Japanese to purchase a 50-mile long drift net.
FAVORITE LURE: The Holy Trinity: bobber, worm, hook.
QUOTE: "There are billions and billions of fish out there and I want to scale every single one."

How To Improve Your Lie

Lying Hints

Fishing is usually fun only after the fact, and only if you can embroider the misery. Here are some lying hints:

- When exaggerating weight, it is handy to remember certain guidelines of reality and, in some cases, good taste. For instance, no one will believe that you caught a 16-pound sunfish. It is also bad taste to conjure up images of a 71-pound carp, even for people you don't like.
- Length is the easiest thing to lie about. If you have caught, for example, a four-pound walleye, but wish to bump up the length, you can always use the old "spawned out" subterfuge. As in, "Yeah, I caught a 26-inch walleye, but she'd just dumped her eggs, so she woulda gone five-and-a-half easy."
- You may lie at will about the degree of difficulty in landing the fish. This is considered socially acceptable and even encouraged, particularly in bass fishing circles: "Yessir, I was dangling the SkitterBuzz from a branch about 40 feet overhead when the bass nailed it in midair. Then the SOB pulled the branch into the water and hung up on a submerged log, so I had to get a chainsaw out to land the sumbitch. When I finally got the sucker in the boat, it slapped my buddy in the face with its tail and dislocated the poor bozo's jaw."
- Lying about the number of fish caught is considered okay if it's a number that can be expressed without scientific notation. Don't say, "I caught 9.0 times 10 to the 5th power." It's a dead giveaway that you're lying. A simple formula to keep in mind when lying about the number of fish is:

  ((x) Number of fish actually caught)+((y) Number of fish hooked but not landed)+((z) Aggregate total of fish landed by other boats near you) ÷ (Number of beers you had while telling story).

Fishing Codependency

How to Fish with Your Dad

If you're like most Norman Rockwell Americans, your dad probably taught you how to fish. He probably took you to some little pond with sunnies and crappies, and you jerked the poor little fish out of the water into perdition. Then, as you got older, he took you on more sophisticated fishing extravaganzas such as bass fishing or drifting for walleyes, or, if your father was a masochist with a strange sense of humor, fly fishing. But, inevitably, there comes a point in a fisherman's life where he believes that his fishing expertise has outstripped his father's.

"The poor old goat," you may mutter patronizingly, "he's just out of the loop on all the latest developments and technological advances in fishing. I'll take him out and show him how the New Man catches fish."

Your dad realizes that his role as fishing master is about to be usurped as you uplink with your mainframe on your Personal Depth Finder/Fish Locating System. You're secretly chortling about blanking the old man.

"Gee, Dad, are you really going to use that Lazy Ike? I mean, that's right out of the 1950s. It's embarrassing. Try one of these grape Gummy Bear-flavored Krankbaits with inset neon graphics."

The old man tells you to kiss his ass and ties on the stupid Lazy Ike, embarrassing you, and almost gratuitously adds that "this baby caught a lot of fish before you were the size of pumpkinseed."

Six hours later, you and your depth finder and your neon grape Gummy Bear lure are 0 for 4 and the old man is making the boat list to starboard because his stringer weighs 29 pounds.

Teaching Your Wife/Girlfriend How to Fish

With the knowledge that this material is inherently sexist, apologies all around, but it is, unfortunately, generally true. There are some caveat here — women who seem genetically predisposed toward being bad fishermen. There are a lot of women who know how to fish; they usually had fathers who taught them how to do it, and let's face it, any yo-yo can fish and usually does. But it places undue strains on one's relationship with a woman when one is forced to teach her how to fish.

Take my wife. Smart. Real smart. Has a college degree and everything. Was a PR manager for a Fortune 250 company, writes, raises our kid like Dr. Spock, and has a fine sense of humor. She also cannot fish. I don't mean won't fish. I mean, *cannot* fish.

I've tried everything. The first time I took her fishing was in Columbus, Ohio, a real fishing mecca if there ever was one. The Scioto and the Olentangy rivers aren't the chalk streams of Scotland or anything, but there are fish in there.

Questions my wife asked on the first trip:

- "Do you actually have to touch the worm?"
- "Doesn't the worm feel the pain of the hook puncturing its innocent little skin?"
- "Do worms scream?"

And so on about the worm. She's hung up on the worm. She doesn't care Shinola about the fish; Save the Goddamn Worm.

So I go into my speed rap about how far down the food chain the worm is and how its central nervous system is about as highly developed as a ballpoint pen and that worms, to my knowledge, do not have any organized religious beliefs.

I then realize that she wants me to bait her hook. While it is a capital crime for a guy to ask another guy to perform this unnatural act, I bait her hook just to cut to the chase.

Hooks baited, we're sitting in the Scioto River in my boat, watching the bobbers. I begin my standard speech on fishing tactics and the life cycle of the fish and how much a good spinning reel costs when her bobber goes under.

"Is the bobber supposed to do that?" she asks plaintively, knowing full well that a fish is on. She is, however, awaiting further instructions from Mission Control.

"Set the hook," I tell her in my best Chuck Yeager voice, letting her know that I'm in full command of the situation. So she jerks back on the hook, and of course there are 70 feet of slack line, but she manages to hook the fish anyway. She then calmly reels the spinning reel backward, sending a few hundred feet of line onto the floor of the boat. I valiantly use a hand over-hand retrieve, which brings an exhausted crappie at bay.

"What's that?" she asks, and I tell her it's a crappie.

"A crappie?" she replies, pronouncing it "crappy."

"Is it a good one?" she asks.

I tell her it's okay. She decides to retire undefeated, until 1984, when I ask her to go trout fishing with me on a small coastal stream in Oregon.

The stream is one of those little dribbles that has about three cutthroat trout per pool. I bait her hook, and she throws the worm — after several concerned questions about its well-being — into the hole. I see her rod arc, and she pulls an 11-inch cutt out of the water like a tuna — no reeling, just a big heave.

"Nice form," I say, noting that it's the biggest trout I've seen come out of the river. I rebait the hook, and she tosses it back in the water. Two seconds later, the rod bends again, she employs the Tuna Retrieve, and the second largest trout I've seen come out of the stream lies stunned on the bank.

"Is that all there is to it?" she says, kind of pointedly.

"Yeah. That's it." I throw my rod in the bushes.

About The Author

J ack Ohman is the editorial cartoonist for *The Oregonian* newspaper in Portland, Oregon. His political cartoons are syndicated in 175 newspapers. This is his fourth book. He is married to Jan Ohman, who is a freelance writer, and they have a son, Eric. Jack Ohman spends too much time writing about fishing and not enough time actually doing it, he claims.